This Messy Entertainment book belongs to:

. . . .

. . . .

Published By Messy Entertainment Ltd 2017
ISBN 978-1-9998015-1-9
Messy Entertainment Ltd
www.messyentertainment.com

My body is really big
and my fins are really wide,
because I am so big
I never try to hide.

ALL ABOUT ME...

Manta Ray

We can grow to be over 6 metres wide

We use gills in our lower body to breathe

A baby Manta Ray is called a pup

Our skeleton is made of cartilage, not bone

We have the largest brain of all fish

We live mainly in the warmest seas, including the Indian, Pacific and Atlantic Oceans.

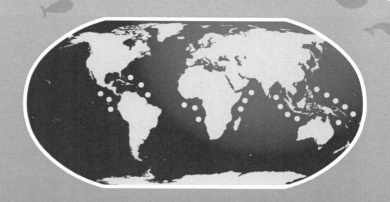

Conservation Status

- Critically Endangered
- Endangered
- Vulnerable
- Near Threatened
- Least Concerned

Manta Rays are considered to be endangered due to habitat destruction and climate change in 2017.

Manta Ray

Can you fill in the missing letters?

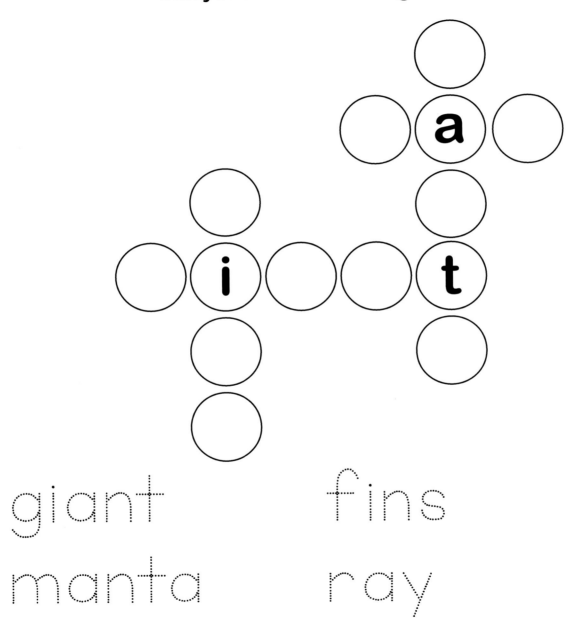

giant
manta

fins
ray

Draw a line to match the animal to its name?

Seahorse

Manta Ray

Jellyfish

Hammerhead
Shark

Can you add together these fish?

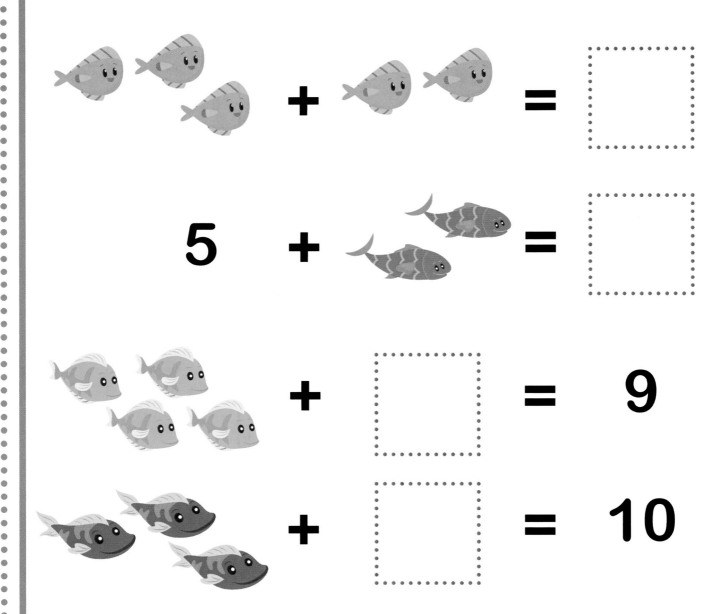

Can you find the way to the reef?

Can you find the way through the maze?

Can you complete this picture by connecting the dots?

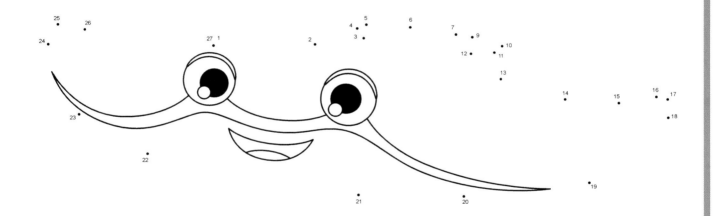

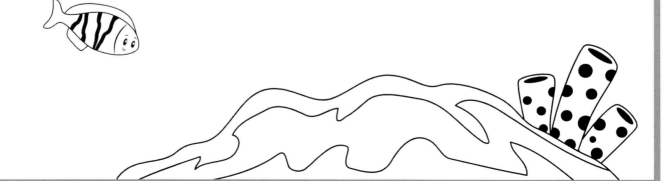

Can you find these words?

MANTARAY   FLAT   FISH   ELEGANT

GLIDE   TAIL   OCEAN   FINS

W	E	R	M	Y	U	O	P
A	F	L	A	T	S	D	F
G	I	H	N	J	K	E	L
Z	N	X	T	A	I	L	C
V	S	B	A	N	K	E	H
M	Q	W	R	E	R	G	S
O	C	E	A	N	T	A	I
Y	U	O	Y	P	L	N	F
R	G	L	I	D	E	T	S

Can you fill in the missing words?

My .... is really long, it helps me to manouvre.

A baby Manta Ray is called a ....

I like to feed on ....

My .... are really wide.

plankton   tail   fins   pup

Manta Ray

Can you find 7 differences?

Can you lead the Manta Ray back to the group?

www.messyentertainment.com

Search 'Messy Entertainment'
for books, apps & much more.